Civic Skills and Values

Sportsmanship

By Dalton Rains

www.littlebluehousebooks.com

Copyright © 2024 by Little Blue House, Mendota Heights, MN 55120. All rights reserved. No part of this book may be reproduced or utilized in any form or by any means without written permission from the publisher.

Little Blue House is distributed by North Star Editions:
sales@northstareditions.com | 888-417-0195

Produced for Little Blue House by Red Line Editorial.

Photographs ©: iStockphoto, cover, 4, 6–7, 10, 18, 20–21, 23, 24 (top left); Shutterstock Images, 8–9, 13, 15, 17, 24 (top right), 24 (bottom left), 24 (bottom right)

Library of Congress Control Number: 2022919926

ISBN
978-1-64619-823-8 (hardcover)
978-1-64619-852-8 (paperback)
978-1-64619-908-2 (ebook pdf)
978-1-64619-881-8 (hosted ebook)

Printed in the United States of America
Mankato, MN
082023

About the Author

Dalton Rains writes and edits nonfiction children's books. He lives in Minnesota.

Table of Contents

Respect the Game **5**

Win or Lose **11**

Fun for All **19**

Glossary **24**

Index **24**

Respect the Game

Sportsmanship is about respect.

It makes games fun.

Sportsmanship happens in many ways.

In some sports, you bow.

In other sports, you shake hands.
This shows respect to others.

Win or Lose

Sportsmanship matters when you win.

Winning is fun.

You can show sportsmanship when you win.
You can give high-fives. This shows respect for the other team.

Sportsmanship also matters when you lose. Losing is hard. You might feel sad.

But sportsmanship still happens.

You always shake hands.

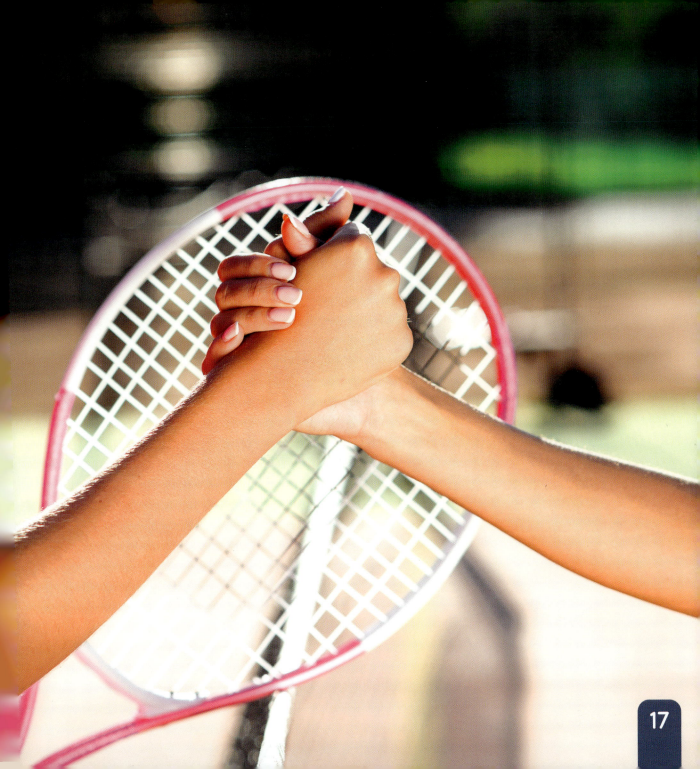

Fun for All

Sportsmanship happens with your teammates.

You help one another.

Sportsmanship happens with other teams. You help players when they are hurt.

You follow the rules and show respect. Sportsmanship helps everyone have fun.

23

Glossary

bow

shake hands

players

team

Index

G
games, 5

L
lose, 14

R
rules, 22

W
win, 11–12